# Table Of Contents

How to get the most out of this book...................................................2
Challenges and Solutions to Understand Reality: ...............................2
A Brief Explanation of Dimensions ....................................................2
The Earth as We have known it...........................................................2
The Lower Perspective: Who were the controllers?............................2
The Secret War on Knowledge ............................................................2
The Internet Trigger.............................................................................2
Atlantis and Lemuria. .........................................................................2
The highest perspective: we are source at play ...................................2
Paving the Way for Living Your Utopia Here On Earth:....................2
Awakening From Slumber: .................................................................2
The 2012 Awakening Catalyst ............................................................2
Emotional Integration .........................................................................2
Closing thoughts on moving forward ..................................................2
Resources.............................................................................................2
Introduction .........................................................................................1

# INTRODUCTION

They say history is written by the victors. Our perceptions of what happened are shaped by the stories we are told, and what we are guided to remember.

We have been told stories of how this Earth was formed, how we got here, how we developed, what came before us, and how it all went down to get to where we are.

For much of my life, I have believed the Earth was created one way. I believed the histories we were told, about how we're at the most civilized time in our society now.

I believed that we were all evolved beings who started as much less intelligent beings. I believed in the stories of vikings and egyptians, of us being this mud and dirt society who only recently discovered and harnessed the power of electricity and atoms.

And yet, something didn't seem quite 'right.'

Like, why was there such a sudden surge of technology in recent years?

Why did multiple cultures reference technology in their stories that seemed to surpass our own?

And even more, why was there so much of my life that was unexplained, the religions that condemned me as a sinner that should spend my life in penance, a god that loved me yet would cast me into hell the moment I slighted him somehow?

And most curious of all, for as far as we have come, for as advanced as we're told to be, and as wonderful as love feels, why do we live with so much fear? Why did it seem like so many beneficial inventions were delayed for so long? We could say greed or corruption, but it seemed strange that they would be so withheld from society.

There was one thing for sure, I was sick of being told what I should chase and what I should feel and what I should believe.

I had a burning desire for truth, burning a fire in my heart/chest. I was going to find the answers any way I could.

These are the questions and passion that drove me to a deep inner search.

This search was conducted through meditations, through mushroom journeys, through mantras, visiting holy sites, visiting nature, doing anything and everything I could to get a glimpse of the truth.

I learned the technique of Kriya Yoga, a breath technique said to be so advanced, you could find ascension/nirvana in this lifetime, bypassing the 'requirement' to spend many lifetimes before you found consciousness.

I struggled for much of my life to 'find the answers.'

In 2015, I experienced a profound inner shift. It wasn't something I did, it was simply one moment I was as I was, the next moment I had a new perspective on life.

For months, I was 'blissed out' - it felt like I was practically floating. The next few years, I gave talks and helped others - and yet, it was hard for me to understand their perspective. I was in such a bliss state, I saw no reason to worry about life.

I decided if I was going to be in this world, it would be key for me to relate and be relatable. I opened my vibration so I could become more grounded in this reality and truly understand and connect with those I was talking with.

As a result, I live between worlds. You might say I'm a modern day shaman. I can interact in this world, and I can sense realities beyond. As such, I've been able to see beyond some of the illusions we have had presented to us in this world.

When I meditate or focus on my third eye, I'm able to 'read' energies. It's like feeling vibrations that I can then interpret into shared meaning.

In this book, I'm going to take you beyond the surface descriptions of what we have been told about reality. Because, if you truly want to understand what's really going on, we're going to go deeper within, and further out than anything you've read before.

Now, if you are here, you are ready to read this. You have evolved your consciousness to a point where this book has reached your hands. These concepts may be a lot to swallow.

However, if you give yourself permission to open up to these possibilities, you are opening your space for expansion. For awareness. For a truly new look at this world, this universe, this reality, and what is really possible for you and for us all in our lifetimes.

We have been playing a 'small' game for too long. We're ready to step forward into our true selves. And one of the first steps, is willingness, and awareness.

Right now, a mass consciousness awakening is going on, and many of us are shaking off our old stories so we can embody and live as who we truly are.

This book is one of the tools intended to help that process of awakening and remembering.

As you read it, you may feel times you want to inquire, times you want to sleep, times to go within.

Trust yourself as you read this, and remember, you have the wisdom within you to take everything in this book and go further within to find your own truths.

Don't just take my word for it. Remember your own wisdom as well.

With love and respect,

Danielle Lynn

# How to get the most out of this book

There are a number of people and sources who have spoken on the nature of reality and the universe. In my own life, I experienced an awakening that shifted me to my core. I experienced a vivid recollection of who I AM that shook me to my core. I became aware of existence on multiple layers. I delved into research, both through inner exploration and exploring materials that felt resonant. This brought me to a new understand of the nature of our universe, of Earth history, of the present, and of where we are headed.

You might say, for a while we've been living in a bubble. And this bubble is about to burst - or rather, it is bursting. This book is one of the signifiers that this is happening.

In the past, we relied on measuring facts in the mind to decide if something was true or not. That time is making way for a more accurate way of knowing truth and getting in tune with what is real, and what is illusion. As you read, it will be important for you to get attuned to what feels resonant with you, and what does not. To do this, it is important to approach this material without judgement, preconceptions, and from a place of an open heart.

The purpose of this book is to open new paths of inner inquiry and exploration. A wayshower for you to investigate what stirs inside of you when you explore these concepts. If this book is able to trigger any sort of peace, remembering, curiosity, or a stir within you even once, then it has done its job. Due to the nature of this subject, I suggest you use this book as springboard for exploration, then to go within with an open heart and discern for yourself "what feels true to me at my very core?"

Sometimes, embracing the truth is uncomfortable at first. There are somethings I will discuss in this book that may not be all flowers and roses. Some things may even seem horrible to comprehend. However, there is no judgement, commendation, or attack in this book. And if anything, we have a bright and exciting present and future ahead of us, for the heavy things mentioned in this book do not have a hold on us anymore - in so much that we now have the power of conscious love, integration, and choice.

There is also much that is not explored within this book, that has happened and is happening in our history, that I may revisit in longer book at a future date. For those chapters, I have included links to resources that have further information if you choose to explore those.

There is a great shift happening at this time. The more we stand in conscious awareness, remembering our unity with all things, the more easeful this shift is for you and all this world.

To our remembering <3

# Challenges and Solutions in Explaining Core Concepts to Understand Reality:

As I mentioned earlier, there are a few challenges and solutions that go hand in hand with exploring reality in this way. Right now, I'm going to address these challenges and provide solutions for us, so we can have an easier time in this experience together.

In the past, I've tuned into my higher consciousness state and shared perspectives. While beautiful and flowery, sometimes they were hard to understand and seemed so complex that some people didn't benefit from them here and now.

So, I chose to explain everything to you Now as simply and clearly as possible.

This book is meant to be an abridged perspective. There are materials and sites that go into deeper details, years, days, timelines. The purpose of this book is to be an introduction into our multidimensional history to help ease the transition of 'waking up' from the amnesia we've been in. I will cite additional resources at the end of the book if you're interested in exploring further.

In this reality, everything is ultimately perspectives. I'm going to share a few perspectives that will help you get clear on some core concepts that our history is built around.

**1) Understanding who you truly are:**

The first thing to understand, is our current, socially accepted limited perception of creation and ourselves.

For as long as you have been alive, you likely have certain perceptions of yourself and of reality. For example, the following is likely:

- You believe you are human or at least have a human body
- You believe you are finite, you live and die
- You believe you are ruled by time
- You believe you are separate from other people, animals, plants and things

Depending on your upbringing or influences, you may also believe:

- There is or isn't a god
- You do or do not reincarnate
- You do or do not have a soul.

If you are reading this, there is a good chance you believe (or believe it is possible) that you have a soul, that there is a greater intelligence to this universe and you are one with it, and that there is more to this reality than meets the eye.

This is closer to the truth. Your human experience is one of many experiences - perhaps even infinite experiences.

Here are some perspectives about who you are that are closer to what we'll call "universal truth", meaning it holds true across many perspectives.

- You are an experience of divinity in a temporary limited body.
- You came here by choice
- You have the ability to create and shape your reality
- You are connected to all that is: All humans, animals plants and all that you see and feel around you and within you are ultimately connected to you and are a part of you.
- You are also in a human experience.

You might wonder how this is so. Where does the idea of a soul fit in? How can I be human AND all of creation?

**One way to explain it is through the Soul Layers. Here is an image representing Soul Layers;**

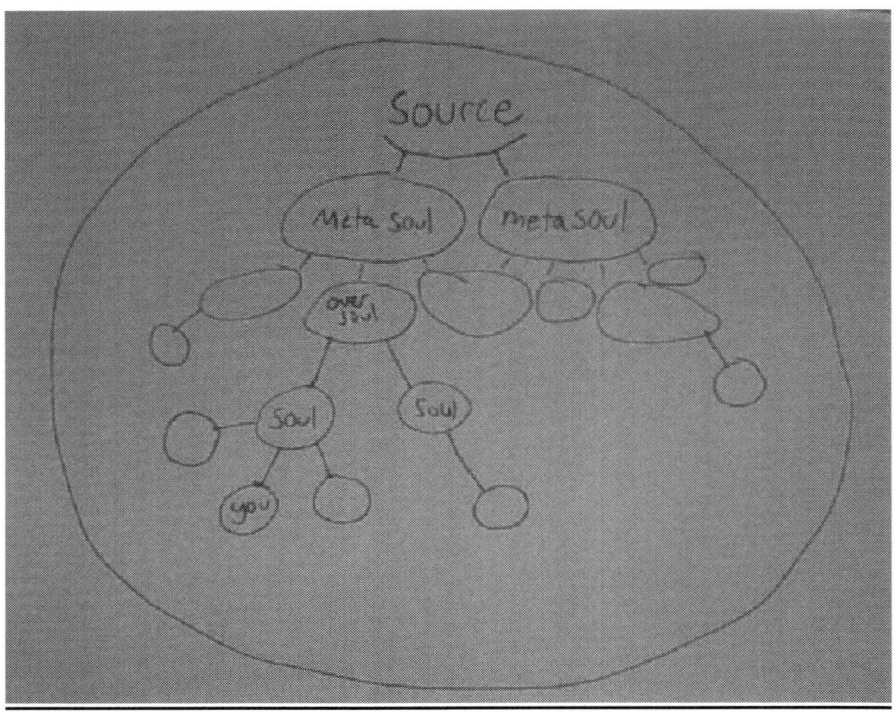

Source - This is all that is, and all we are. As you can see, it is labeled at the top, but it's not really closed off from anything else, because source itself is the bubble that everything IS contained in. So we are source, that is within source, pretending to be other things.

MetaSoul - This is the first 'split' from source consciousness. The "Yin-Yang" Seeds of the universe and creative forces.

(Additional layers) - ? - When I tune in, I feel 'other layers' that aren't represented here in this picture. I feel that there is some additional information when you view this multidimensionally. So when you view this picture, understand that there is additional layers here not being visually represented.

OverSoul - This would be our higher dimensional selves. Depending on the dimension it may have an individual appearance or a collective of souls being a unity. If you are familiar with the work of Abraham Hicks, the entity known as Abraham would likely fit in around here (and around the additional layers). When you find soul family, you're often looking here. Some soul mate connections.

Soul - This is our energetic self, often existing in the astral. Your soul can have multiple lifetime instances running simultaneously. Deep soulmate connections, possible twin flame experiences.

You in your experience now - This is the focused consciousness of you here and now.

?? - There are microcosm layers to you as well that point back to source not represented here in this picture, that make this representation look and feel more like an infinity loop.

**This is just one representation of ourselves**

Now, this image is presented as though its a hierarchy, but in reality, it functions more like a web that connects back on itself, or an energy field fractal.

The you and experience you are having that is here is reflected infinitely smaller and infinitely larger. What you feel is reflected in your fuller self, and deep within you.

Sometimes, you will find groups or people who have similar views, ideas, ideals, perspectives. These are often soul family groups or meta soul groups.

Often times, we feel these deep connections with people, because we can see and feel our fuller selves in them. As we said, ultimately, we are ALL connected, however, those who feel closer in proximity to us will often trigger greater feelings of closeness, until we are universal consciousness.

We tend to think of ourselves as individuals, but our oversouls and metasouls are more like collectives - how you might see bees or ants or schools of fish - seemingly separate entities that work together as an organism.

And if you go further out, you'll see all meta souls are really a collective of source - and all of creation is one whole being-ness. .

This is what religions, spiritual teachers, and philosophical texts mean when they say 'we are all one.'

Because in reality, we ARE oneness, that is having a temporary experience of separation for the sake of experiencing itself.

This is why one of the most true ways for any of us to describe ourselves as I AM.

**That may be a lot to process. It's alright to take a moment to integrate that**. If you don't fully understand all that was said, or you sort of get it but have a hard time really experiencing it, that is perfectly okay. For most of us, it was irrelevant to know that truth while we're in the human body. We have come into human bodies to experience the joy of creation through one perspective. You are awakening to your multidimensional nature, naturally. You don't have to pick it apart with your mind. Multidimensionality is a state that is beyond the mind. If it is important for you to 'get it' while you're here in your human experience, you will 'get it' effortlessly at the synchronous moment, there's nothing to force or do.

Remember, whether you're experiencing life as a human, or whether you are seeing things from a universal state, understand it's just another way of experiencing life. Flying in a plane gives you one view on life, versus driving in a car, versus walking on foot. They are not better or worse experiences over all. Each have their 'pros and cons.' The plane is faster and you see farther. The car gives a sense of speed and you experience winding roads while still moving fast. The foot traveling is slower but there's a richness and fullness in the direct experience of connecting with the world around you.

In the same way, different experiences of life will be felt differently by you depending on your perspective, whether you're experiencing it as a human, or an awakened human, or perhaps in your higher consciousness awareness.

## 2) You are a multidimensional being.

This means, you exist in multiple realities and levels of consciousness simultaneously -whether you're constantly aware of it or not.

This means, you occupy, you exist in, and ultimately, you are, more than one dimension of existence.

An easy way to understand this is what happens when you dream. When you dream, are you truly someone else or somewhere else? It can certainly feel that way while you're dreaming. However, you are also asleep in your bed, your body is laying down. You are simultaneously having an experience of moving around and interacting, while another aspect of you is asleep and unconscious.

In a similar way, when you are waking and walking around as a human, there is that aspect of you, and then there is the soul aspect of you that is conscious on another level. There is a collective consciousness level that is you as well - and so forth.

We tend to think of ourselves as individuals, but our oversouls and metasouls are more like collectives - how you might see bees or ants or schools of fish - seemingly separate entities that work together as an organism.

And if you go further out, you'll see all meta souls are really a collective of source - and all of creation is one whole being-ness.

This is what religions, spiritual teachers, and philosophical texts mean when they say 'we are all one.'

Because in reality, we ARE oneness, that is having a temporary experience of separation for the sake of experiencing itself.

This is why one of the most true ways for any of us to describe ourselves as I AM.

In a later chapter in this book, I go into understanding the dimensions in further detail

**3) Reality is not really Linear, it is more of a Fractal**

We experience a lot of our lives thinking we're moving from point A to point B in a straight line. We think there's a start and a finish. Reality is much more cyclical, like a spiral. It goes infinitely deeper, and expands infinitely farther.

One clear way to understand reality is to Imagine that all of creation is a fractal. A fractal is a never ending pattern, often seen as a curve or geometric figure, that goes infinitely deeper and farther in all directions, each part of which has the same statistical character as the whole.

Here is an example of a fractal:

As you can see, it continues to get smaller and smaller, as well as larger and larger. However, no matter how small or large it gets, the core image continually remains the same.

(You can see a moving example of a fractal here: ( http:/fractalfoundation.org/resources/what-are-fractals/)

Earlier, when we were talking about oversouls and metasouls, a clear imagery to imagine is yourself, and all of your soul lineage as one aspect of a fractal connected to the whole.

All of source is the whole fractal, and a single spiral is an oversoul, and an offshoot of that spiral is a branching of that oversoul, an offshoot meta soul, an offshoot soul, an offshoot individual, and so forth.

What you may notice, and what makes fractals fascinating, is they get infinitely smaller and infinitely larger, but the same identical pattern is present in all offshoots of the fractal, no matter how far you zoom in, or how far you zoom out. This is a parallel of our multidimensional nature.

## 4) We are Living Libraries: Our DNA is a microcosm of all of creation

Each of us has DNA, a blueprint not just of our bodies, but of all the data of the universe. Our DNA is like the microcosm of who we are, and all that has been.

We marvel at computers and the information they contain. Our DNA contains the blueprint for all of life. You might say, we are a complete blueprint of the universe and all of creation, holding a complete blueprint of the universe and all of creation, contained in a complete blueprint of the universe and all of creation, infinitely in all directions.

Your DNA is an active key. It can be modified, decoded, accessed, altered. It is some of the most advanced biological technology that exists. When we say technology, we don't mean AI or implants, we mean universal structure technology.

It is a living library so complex, that fabled libraries such as the Library of Alexandria wouldn't even come close to scratching the surface of information DNA has.

DNA is also resilient. It can travel safely through and beyond space and time. All that we are and ever have been is connected to this framework. And we are linked through consciousness that is also accessible via DNA sequencing.

DNA is multidimensional, in its information. It contains blueprints that create physical outputs as well as energetic upgrades.

Your DNA is activating and awakening at this time.

In an article that discusses why DNA activation is important,

In 4D [Human dimensionality], you have two DNA strands [loops or toroids]. Those who would tell you that you have 12 are giving you a 4D description of a multidimensional puzzle... The individual who has embodied twelve strands of DNA or has become "Christed" moves beyond limitation within human form. In moving beyond limitation, the individual also moves out of fear. As all of mankind embodies the new genetics, civilization will gradually restructure itself to be based on unconditional love.

You can read the full article on DNA activation here: http://in5d.com/dna-activation-upgrade-and-ascension/

Additionally, we will mention that DNA activation from this perspective is not something you have to 'think about' or 'do' or 'make happen' at this juncture. There was a time when it was necessary, however right now we are experiencing a mass awakening, that includes our DNA awakening.

To streamline this process, accept, love, and integrate everything that emerges right now - the good and the ugly as it were. This is the way you can help your process the most.

## 5) Sacred Geometry Reflects to Us The Building Blocks of Reality

Our DNA, repeating patterns, and fractals also correlate to sacred geometry - or the building blocks of the universe.

Sacred geometry is the study of the naturally occurring mathematical formations that are the building blocks of the universe. We see sacred geometry form naturally in nature, from the spiral shells and succulent plants, to the very spiral of our galaxies.

The fibonacci sequence (shown below) is a common sacred geometry sequence, where series of numbers in which each number ( Fibonacci number ) is the sum of the two preceding numbers. The simplest is the series 1, 1, 2, 3, 5, 8, and so forth.

This is the visual representation

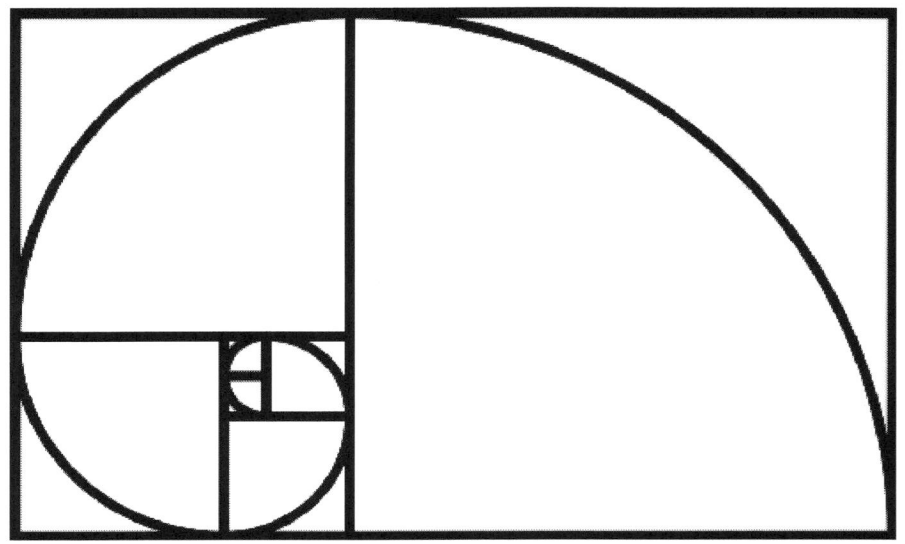

Notice the parallel with the spiral and fractal?

What makes this sequence so fascinating is how it is repeated in nature

Notice how sacred geometry parallels the fractal reality mentioned earlier in this chapter.

We create using vibrational sacred geometry patterns. Sometimes we construct concepts to try to understand this with our mind - such as 'the law of attraction.'

## 6) We are constructing reality from the inside out - based on the way we focus our energy

We are internal to external creators.

What many of us don't currently see or remember, is we exist as a light matrix pattern, or energy/vibration, which then reflects outwards into our reality. Our body, our life situations, our thoughts, our feelings, these are all a reflection of that inner space, moment to moment.

Some people call this a 'light body.' Some people call it an inner matrix or grid. Sometimes, you hear references to Chakras, which are known as the 'hubs' of the inner light matrix. They're hubs, because they can sometimes become bottlenecks for energy when not allowed to flow.

We are able to augment these patterns, our light bodies, and our experiences of reality. However, much of this knowledge on how to do this has been temporarily lost to us, unless you join a secret society, or learn from a specific teacher. That is, until now. This knowledge is once again able to be open and available to all, freely.

In the past, we have used breath techniques, meditation, mantras, and so forth to augment our states.

Currently, at the time of writing this book, the most powerful way we can access our awareness of our light body matrix is to integrate all of our current experiences and feelings without judgement, both the seemingly 'good and bad.' By integrating, with unconditional love, we open our inner access and step into our awareness as 'masters of our matrix'

It's key to understand that you are no victim of the circumstances of life. Even when going through great challenges or suffering. You are a conscious creator who chose a temporary situation for the sake of an experience.

That doesn't mean you need to 'blame' yourself for suffering. What it does mean, is the more you take responsibility for embracing and allowing how you feel and how you focus, you will be able to shift the trajectory of your energy and experiences in the Now.

In other books and materials of mine, I explore this subject in more detail. I suggest you subscribe to receive my newsletter (at https://www.daniellelynn.com) and I'll connect you with those books and resources.

For now, It is enough to remember, you came forward as a conscious creator, and you came here by choice for a reason, you are more than your human body, and you are connected to all of creation directly.

**7) Time is an illusion and a construct created for the mind**

We have lived within a space and time model... for a 'while' now here on Earth.

Ultimately, the concepts of Space and Time are all relative. Time and space is a tool for the mind to use to create a simulated experience of 'movement' or 'the passage' of an experience.

However, who you are is a consciousness that is aware beyond the confines of the mind.

Ultimately, there is no time, because everything is actually happening Now.

NOW and Not-Now are the only two states that exist (And even then, that's all relative).

With these understandings, concepts like past lives become more like 'parallel' lives: experiences that are existing simultaneously in an overlay on us now, at another frequency.

The idea is similar to how AM and FM radio waves can occupy the same space.

I go into detail on how to see time as an illusion on my post here:

https://daniellelynn.com/how-to-see-time-as-an-illusion-part-1/

## 8) Your Mind isn't the wisdom center in your body, it is your heart

We've given the mind a very heavy job of 'being' us.

Yet, it wasn't created for that purpose. The mind is an analyzing tool. THe heart is meant to be the main 'control panel' of the small self existence.

When we work primarily from the heart, with the mind and gut being 'accessories' to the heart, we find more balance in our thoughts, actions, feelings, and choices.

So, how do we tune in to heart-centered consciousness?

You are intelligence and wisdom beyond the mind. Imagine your heart is this intelligent processor. As you read information, this this information in with your heart - almost envision it processing into your heart, then spreading to your mind and your intuitive gut.

As you do this, you will experience a sensation. The sensation will either feel like expansion and being able to breathe easily, or it will feel closer to contraction and having your breath closed off.

If it is truth, it feels more like expansion. If it feels like contraction, it is more than likely not resonant with you.

However, for this to effectively work, you must keep your heart clear from bias. The more biased we are, the more that signal reflects your own constrictions, rather than unbiased truth.

You can keep a clear heart by stating "I wish to know the full truth from the neutral zero point perspective." Continue to say that until you feel the neutrality within you. Then say "Show me what truth feels like" and feel it. Then say "Show me what not truth feels like" and feel that. From that point, you can use your heart as a detection.

If you come across something that constricts, sit with it in awareness. It will reveal to you on its own whether it is a personal bias or whether it is indicating to you something that is not aligned with all that is.

As they say, the more you use it, the more you will fine tune this process and it will become part of your nature.

With your heart as the receiving point, you will find balance, and even a deeper understanding as you progress with this book - and really with all things in life if you choose to continue to utilize this new way of looking at life.

## 9) Paradoxes point you to deeper truth

One way we know the mind was not meant to be our primary processing source is it's inability to grasp the power of paradoxes.

Paradoxes are often seen by the mind as nuisances. They're often unanswerable by simple logic.

That is because a paradox points to a dimension that exists beyond the mind.

A paradox can point to two things being true at once. Such as we can have a 'past life' where we existed in roman times, and at the same time, that life is existing simultaneously with us right now.

To the mind, this makes no sense. That happened hundreds, thousands of years ago! It says. However, from a fuller perspective, everything is happening right Now. When you understand the fractal nature of reality, and the awareness that time is an illusion, you can conceivably experience that 'past' life right now, if you were to focus your awareness on yourself in a higher state of awareness, say 7th dimensional consciousness for example.

As you start to embrace paradoxes rather than feeling perplexed by them, you open yourself up to the multidimensional nature of things.

You can be highly advanced soul, and be stumbling around in your human life.

You can be aware and asleep.

All thing can exist simultaneously, while nothing exists at all.

Paradoxes embrace duality while simultaneously bring us beyond duality, which lives only in the lower dimensions, and connects us to the wholeness we are.

For now, I suggest meditating on the following: "Even if my mind doesn't understand paradoxes, my heart does. And I open myself up to the portal that paradoxes provide me into deeper knowing."

# A Brief Explanation of Dimensions

Understanding dimensions and how it can skew our perception is important for understanding the information in this book. So we're going to briefly cover this right now.

**So what are the dimensions of consciousness?**

The dimensions of consciousness are not a time or a place, but a state or way of BE-ing.

When we meditate, we attempt to connect with certain states of consciousness, usually higher states of consciousness.

For the sake of this book we might say there are 12 dimensions. For the sake of reality, we'd say there are infinite dimensions as well as one.

**Here is a brief description of 12 of the main dimensions:**

(Note, this is an abridged explanation of a deeper dimensional study, with some of my own takes on it, that I found to be highly accurate, You can find the full study here:

http://illuminology.tumblr.com/post/55526706444/the-12-dimensions-explained

### *The Twelfth Dimension ~ The All That Is; The Source*

There are no "me's," "you's," or "us's." It is absurd to say, "I am [this] God," because at this level there is no "I" to say it.

### *The Eleventh Dimension ~ The Yin Yang*

This is where source first 'splits.' It creates the masculine and feminine energy. The Yin-Yang is a solid representation of this. There is the Yin with a little Yang in it, There is Yang with a little yin in it.

The two energies are polarized, light and dark, and yet, within each they contain the seed of the other. They are never truly separate. Charged by the push and pull, they swirl together, a cosmic force.

## *The Tenth Dimension ~ The Universe*

The 10th Dimension is considered a conscious universal entity without form. Born of the union spark that occurs at the 11th dimension, it is a 'seed of life'. This is considered to be what happens when Yin and Yang mix. It is the stage that is set for form, and within it a blueprint of all possibilities that can exist within form.

## *The Ninth Dimension ~ Form and Hierarchy*

The Ninth Dimension is where form occurs. Before this point, there is formlessness. At this place, an entity could choose to take form. You could see entities being planets and star systems in this dimension.

This is also said to be where hierarchy for form is created. The grass needs the Earth to live, The Earth needs the sun to live, the sun needs the universe to live.

## *The Eighth Dimension ~ Group Souls (Oceans of Light)*

At this dimension, a collection of entities works together as one being. This is similar to a school of fish, a hive of bees, or perhaps even a single body.

Each 'individual' soul would have a unique yet integral function.

## *The Seventh Dimension ~ The Rainbow Dimensional Explorers*

There are many forms seventh dimensional beings can take. Beautiful, rainbow webs, vortexes, swirls are what they would appear like to us. These beings would explore the dimensions (as mentioned earlier in this book, there are dimensions 'beyond' the 12 represented here)

### The Sixth Dimension ~ The Communication Dimension

Relating to our throat chakra, this dimension is all about taking in information, and being able to communicate it effectively. This is where we create symbols, symbology that are understood across dimensions. DNA as we know it was created at this dimension of awareness. The Akashic Records (which are the complete files on everyone and everything) are also found here.

### The Fifth Dimension ~ The Higher Astral Plane

When religions talk about heaven, this is the plane they are referring to. There is no gender here, rather, we take form androgynously as light bodies.

This is a place of peace, without suffering, where actions are based on love.

### The Fourth Dimension ~ The Lower Astral Plane

You might see this place as a sort of a gray area. You can experience forms of 'heaven, purgatory, and hell' here. It's a polarized place, meaning where there is light and dark, good and bad, right and wrong.

This is the center point of physical creation. We can choose to go further up or further lower. In our bodies, this is our location of the heart.

The principles of karma, time travel, luck, psychic surgery, flying, astral travel, are all explored here.

### The Third Dimension ~ Physical "Reality"

This is the realm of choice. We can act like angels or act like demons. When we base our actions entirely on 'what we see' we end up living by the rules of the material world. When we do this, it becomes impossible for 'magic' to connect with us, as we have decided to abide by 'material laws.'

The EGO thrives at the third dimensional level. It is awareness of the 'little self' and seeing oneself as separate from all things.

This is also the realm that logic rules.

## *The Second Dimension ~ Animals and Biology*

Second dimensional consciousness is awareness on a biological level. This is where we connected with the animal and plant kingdoms.

Our bodies function autonomously at a 2 dimensional level. We connect to animalistic sexual creative forces at the second dimension.

There is many different beings that exist on this level. Fairies, devas, nature spirits, chemical beings, elementals and also the demonic energies.

The creation Dragons can also be connected with on this level.

## *The First Dimension ~ Realm of Quantum Physics, Microcosms and Macrocosms*

Here we find consciousness in the 'inanimate.'

Many humans believe minerals and plants do not have consciousness, and yet they are thriving with energy and conscious awareness, right to the very core of the atom.

When we connect with this level we connect with the entire physical world on a molecule level. This is the place of quantum physics a place of electrons, protons, nuclei, and quarks. It is the gateway between the macrocosm and the microcosm.

This is why it's so important to not 'judge' the levels of consciousness as being desirable or undesirable. Every level has its function in the whole. We made this mistake once in an ancient time. This time, we remember, to embrace the whole.

You can find spider consciousness on this level. As they are the guardians of the matrix of Gaia's consciousness.

~~~

**Why do we see things differently depending on what dimension we are in?**

The best example we can share right now is the following:

One way to visualize how this works, is how different an object looks depending on what dimension you're looking at it in.

For example, we can look at the map of earth as flat, or we can look at the earth as a sphere. They look vastly different, depending on the dimension you are seeing them in.

Below is a 2D (flat) representation)

And this is a 3D representation. Notice how it changes the perspective on how the image is laid out and how everything comes together.

Your perspective, and which dimension you are looking at an experience from, will alter your view and experience of it.

**Much of our current reality had been experienced on the 3rd Dimensional level in our recent human history.**

Recently, this has shifted considerably. We have shifted from the 4th to a more 5th Dimensional consciousness - or at least the Earth has. And this is part of the reason so much is changing within you, and around you. (we will delve into this topic of the current shift later in the book)

Our history has happened multidimensionally as well, and one reason so much seems hidden from us, is when we forget our multidimensional nature, it can be challenging to remember, let alone process, what has happened and what is happening. However, we are all up to the challenge, and the more we allow ourselves to naturally engage with who we are, the more ease we find with connecting to this knowledge.

Again, this is what this book is choosing to address and help you remember.

Remember, multidimensional understanding has limits within the mind. We can show a representation of a 3d object by drawing on a 2d plane, but we then have trouble interacting with its 3d nature, as we cannot spin it and experience its depth, until we go beyond the 2d plane.

In a similar way, we can explain the multiple dimensions here, but our minds can only process a concept of the dimensions.

In order to understand this, and much of the content in the book, I suggest using heart centered consciousness.

This can be as simple as focusing your energy in your heart space, and sitting in awareness with yourself, listening and feeling for what arises as you connect with a topic.

**Get your Multidimensional pantsuit and cape, We are ready to delve deeper**

Now that you have an understanding of your multidimensional nature and your newly remembered skillset of tuning in with your heart/gut/mind in unison, we are ready for exploring your true history of the universe and specifically, what truly happened multidimensionally that brought us here and now.

# The Earth as We have known it, until now

The Earth as we know it was explained to have been formed about 4.6 billion years ago. We were told there were many cycles of evolution. There were dinosaurs, ice ages, cavemen, and then very recently, there was advancement and modern civilization.

We have been told our evolution is linear and moves upwards in time. In recent history, we've been told we discovered fantastic inventions that have jetted us into a newer age of technology and advancement.

For all intents and purposes, we are told that the current time in human history is the time where we are most advanced and prosperous.

But is that so?

What we have not been told, is tens of thousands of years ago, we had technology that could instantly heal, unlimited energy, and more.

We lived in a time where automation handled everything, and life was a paradise.

There were weapons that could target minds, of mass destruction.

Science and medicine so advanced, that there were no diseases, and humans could live for hundreds of years - and beyond.

So what happened? And if that's true, where are the remnants of the culture?

The answer is, the victors are the ones who write - or rewrite - our history.

However, the truth can be hidden for a while, but not forever.

As we are awakening, we're connecting with trigger points of remembering.

And in exploring our TRUE history, we are casting off the 'slave history' that was fed to us, and embracing the truth.

This process may feel intense as we awaken, but know that in embracing our truth, we will be able to step in our power, and choose the creation of our lives, truly.

Let's begin.

**The true history of Earth, right under our nose in Microcosm**

Have you ever been fascinated by North Korea? North Korea, is the upper half of Korea. In the 50's it was split off by war. THe upper half was communist run, the lower half was supported by americans.

Over the course of the war, the split remained permanent. 50 years later, and we still have 2 Koreas.

Here's the interesting part.... Since that time, South Korea is a modern day civilization, comparable to western worlds.

North Korea however, has been under a dictatorship that treats their leaders like a deity, sends political dissidents to prison camps, has mass starvation, little technology, and is told daily that they are 'at war' with the USA - who they claim cowers in fear of North Korea.

It's fascinating, because North Korea is a country frozen in 50's soviet era time, closed off from the world, and told that they are living in a Utopia while being surrounded by starving people, lack of basic human necessities for the masses while the heads of the country have luxuries, and the people are taught to live in fear.

So, what if I were to say this whole world is in a 'North Korea" situation? Or at least, it is in a situation where it was North Korea and is just now freed and on the brink of 'reentering' civilization?

I would say it's fairly accurate.

**Earth is having a similar parallel - And knowledge has been purposefully hidden until now.**

Earlier, I spoke on fractals. North Korea is a fractal representation of what is going on now.

Earth has been told that it is currently at the most advanced stage it has ever reached, that those that came before us were all cavemen or less advanced.

And yet the truth is far from this.

**We have Existed as War Prisoners, Without Even Realizing**

Remember how we spoke earlier on Light body matrixes?

When we're connected naturally with the earth, we grow, evolve and thrive in accordance with natural law, through our bodies and light bodies.

A sort of 'soul cycle' occurs naturally, on the planet, as bodies, and within our energy fields.

It is a nourishing, sustaining ecosystem across dimensions, a natural and organic light matrix.

However, at some point in the experience, that natural matrix and connection was hijacked.

A group of entity 'controllers' stepped in. From a human perspective, we'd see these as aliens. From a multidimensional perspective, they were polarized dark beings with a focus on 'power over others.'

They created a 'false inorganic matrix grid' that overlaid the natural grid. They then trapped the energy of beings (such as humans) on this grid to harvest energy through deception. It sounds similar to the Matrix, doesn't it.

Instead of naturally progressing, these souls were placed in 'false karma cycles' that kept them distracted and constantly struggling against themselves lifetime after lifetime.

Instead of benefiting from our natural grown and energy fields, those who were 'trapped' in this grid had their energy syphoned off, their lives artificially shortened, and their awareness purposely redirected or misdirected.

Programs were set into place to keep humans from self discovery. Some false churches and religions were made, focused on keeping people in fear of an 'angry god' and how they were sinners, other programs focused on constant wars.

This was a form of energetic rape, of our souls and of the planet Earth.

This is not something I say lightly. It is what it is. And this may be one of the greater shocks people experience as they awaken. It is not necessary to dwell on this, however, self love, non judgement, forgiveness and unity consciousness are all key as you integrate and awaken.

It is inevitable that this truth will reach the masses in a way where it becomes common knowledge. Again, imagine what it would take to integrate the people of North Korea back into 'modern society.'

It will be up to each of us to hold a space of loving forgiveness and transmutation, so that we can use this experience as a springboard of evolution, instead of turning back into war and pain.

# Who were these controllers and what did they want? Why did they do this?

This is a multidimensional question, with a multidimensional answer.

From the lower perspectives, this was a group of beings, including several races of alien species who wanted a slave race they could control.

They worked on principles of deception, to create a 'prison planet colony' with hopes that they could create a system that self-perpetuated oppression through the following:

1. Divide and Conquer - Think competitive 'us versus them' sports and politics

2. Victim/Victimizer - Hero worship culture and teaching people learned helplessness

3. Sexual Abuse and Sexual Misery - Teaching sex is bad in religions, making people feel like sinners for sexual urges, shaming females for sexual feelings, shaming males for not being sexual enough.

4. Child Abuse - Conforming children, cutting them off from joy and creativity, sending them to inspiration killing schools

5. Misogyny - the fight of men versus women, which keeps the energy divided.

All these things were normalized in our western society, and in societies across the world. Yet, from our very core, we are joy and unconditional love.

We are taught to work against our natural power and energy, so that we can turn ourselves against ourselves, and which keeps us from 'waking up.'

Of course, that is how it WAS.

If you are reading this and feel shocked, know that it is important to tend to any feelings you have about this. Your feelings are valid. Know however, you are far from powerless. And while this was once the case, the old power structure that was in place is no more.

The false grids, at the time of writing this book, have already been severed. They are no longer functioning. If they appear to be, it's much like a chicken with its head cut off, still running around. It will not sustain itself any longer.

All new souls who are being born to the earth at this time are being connected to the natural light grid of Earth. We who are here and were born before that time are also being provided opportunities to directly connect to our natural grid source. This may be why, especially in recent times, you have 'changed dramatically' and find yourself drawn to new people and circumstances.

We are a people who were once kept in the dark, experiencing an eclipse in our consciousness, now stepping forward into the light of our newly remembered awareness.

**Yes, Aliens live amongst us.**

Yes, aliens have and do live among us, sometimes in plain sight. Some wear human skinsuits. Some are born as humans. Many of them are at dimensional frequencies that were too fine for the human eye to perceive. If a person has their third eye opened, they could pick them out of a crowd, or sense them in the atmosphere.

Aliens range from loving, to neutral, to destructive - just as humans do. There is nothing to fear from aliens here and now, especially as you work within the frequency of your heart.

Know that they cannot harm you without your express permission to work with them.

Some of us who were born here are 'alien' souls who spent many incarnations in other planets and dimensions, who then chose to be born this life in human bodies. Meaning we came from other dimensions and places at this exact moment in human history to help with the ascension. If this sparks something within you, you reading this may notice you're 'unusual' and have always been slightly above pace. You may have even looked to the sky now and then and felt a yearning to go 'home.' This is an indication that you indeed have come from another 'place and time' to assist. And we thank you.

As we move forward into our awareness, we have alien allies and family who are eager and excited to connect with us here on Earth.

Note that for those who say "where is the proof" realize that fish below the surface have a hard time 'seeing' the people who are looking in at them from the pond. As we wake up to our multidimensional awareness through embodiment, you will begin to see this world in a new light. Many things once hidden will reveal themselves to you.

There are no more secrets, it's simply a matter of choice - are you choosing to see truth? Sometimes this requires the 'death' of the way you once saw life, and there is no turning back.

This is why some of us choose ignorance over knowing. For some, the idea of everything they once knew being false is too jarring to consider or comprehend.

Know that no matter what, when you choose from a space of love, you will always experience that which is most beneficial to you in the moment. Never worry about 'missing out' Remember, time is all relative. Focus on the moment in a state of allowing and love for all you are now.

**So what did they want?**

The simple answer is they wanted to survive. They saw the enslavement and entrapment of the earth and her people as their vehicle to survival.

Our DNA is also a factor. Many of these races see the human DNA as seed DNA. Able to work with many different codes, for some aliens on the brink of extinction, human DNA contained the DNA codes of all the galaxy, and a possible solution to their problem.

It's important to note, that we were not alone, and have had benevolent beings assisting us as well through this process.

Indeed, the current ascension is a creation set in motion by a collective of beings who chose to assist the Earth from this entrapment, and could see beyond time that this particular 'moment' was the key point where a major catalyst could occur.

# The Secret War on Knowledge - Keeping a race of slaves

Until the recent introduction of the internet, much of our knowledge has been kept under lock and key - almost literally.

Only secret societies, the wealthy, the powerful had knowledge, understanding, and access to what truly is. This was part of the original control programming, intended to keep humans ignorant.

The main reason being, if a society could be controlled and guided on what to focus on, they could be easily harvested and harnessed towards whatever goals the controller was interested in.

Those who would question what the controllers wanted were cast out, or labeled as crazy.

The idea of a conspiracy theorist arose, and anyone attempting to question the norms of reality are quickly mocked and quieted.

False stories and theories were mixed in with legitimate ones.

Notice without bias, how often 'crackpot theories' are put down so people do not question their reality. It's important to note, that not ALL theories are true, which is why discernment is key to know what is relevant and what is a red herring.

In an already complex reality, it made it feel nearly impossible to discern what was true and what was not - at least from the 3D perspective.

**Control through false religion**

Note, I am not naming any religions in this section. It is up to you to decide if a religion is false or heart-aligned by using your own discernment.

False Religions were introduced alongside Truth-pointing Religions built around love. False-religions use pain and fear to scare and control members into compliance. Truth-pointing religions teach open-hearted acceptance, love for all, and self awareness through inner inquiry. They also teach that the religion or training is only one step on the path, not the destination, and that it is up to the individual to awaken to the divinity within.

Ultimately, all religions are not meant to be an end goal, they are meant to be one phase of experience. Just as we graduate school, we graduate from our religions once we distill and integrate the lessons.

Other notable sources of control happened through the channels of:

- Food modifications
- Over-sexualization of women
- Oer-masculinization of men
- Terrorism (physical and psychological)
- Media bias
- Programmed Entertainment

# The Internet was suppose to destroy us and instead paved the way to freedom.

One of the greatest inventions of our time, was the introduction of the internet.

It's somewhat of an ironic achievement, as the internet was intended to be the ultimate control and monitoring structure. It was intended that we would be monitored and have tabs kept on us at all times.

While that has happened to a certain extent, what was unexpected was the deluge of free information that swept across the internet. It allowed soulmates and soul family to efficiently find each other and connect across continents and without troubling themselves over distance.

It allowed for the sharing of information that revealed the great secrets of the mystery schools, secret societies, and other information that was hidden from the public.

It also created an artificial network that mimicked and mirrored the 'lightworker/wayshower grid', that allowed them to effectively share ideas that instigated the tipping point of mass consciousness.

In other words, the internet helped us solidify our ascension path by making information readily available, and by our choice to focus on connecting with inner truths, rather than being told what to believe.

You might say, the 'wayshowers', as you and I are known, came forward at this time of internet creation, to 'hijack' the tool that would have been meant for our destruction, and instead shifted the energy to create the tipping point for ascension.

And yes, this has already happened Now.

So, what brought us to this Now point? How did we 'know' to come here and now to tip the consciousness scale? (Remember, we work multidimensionally, and beyond space and time, our human experiences are only a fraction of our whole experience)

Many of us wayshowers who are here, remember other attempts we had at raising the consciousness level of this planet. Two of the notable instances where in our lifetimes in

# Atlantis and Lemuria.

## The Trigger Point of Atlantis and Lemuria:

In current days, you know Atlantis and Lemuria as ancient civilizations, perhaps as myths or legends. You probably heard of Atlantis falling below the sea. Lemuria may have reminded you of crystals.

From the perspective of linear time, both of these civilizations are 'ancient' - Lemuria existed roughly 50,000 years ago, Atlantis roughly 20,000 years ago, right around the fall of the silver age into the bronze age.

These civilizations have many parallels to each other. The technology and awareness was so that some beings could even 'travel beyond time' between civilizations.

Each of these civilizations was a height of achievement at the time for humanity. In Lemuria, they discovered crystal technology. It was a highly evolved place, where there were beautiful gardens, and people were nurtured and encouraged to live as was true to them. Crystal libraries and technology were used here. It was technology in symbiosis with all of nature. There was a heavy emphasis on emotions. This eventually became one of the elements that contributed to their downfall, as focusing only on emotions ultimately lead to an imbalance.

Atlantis was the 'response' to this imbalance. It was a place of high spiritual advancement. Spiritual advancement and reaching and connecting with high levels of consciousness was highly prized and focused on. They utilized crystalline technologies as well. There were not 'rulers' or 'governments' quite how we know it, but there were stewards and councils of the people, for the people. Being a 'spiritual scientist' was a highly revered profession. And all those who would be in positions that were considered powerful, saw themselves truly as equals to all people in service of all. That is, until the ego began to sway a few, then a few more. Just as in Lemuria, Atlantis had an imbalance as well: there was a sense of detachment, having departed from the Lemurian emotional focus. Beings started to 'forget' they were connected to the whole and made choices of power over others, turning the once beneficial technology into weapons. Millions of lives were wiped out. This too, eventually contributed to the fall of Atlantis.

Each of these civilizations was an 'experiment' in creating the ultimate catalyst of awakening. You who is reading this book lived in one or both of these civilizations - or you visited them at one time or another.

You are likely going through a 'healing' of sorts related to that time.

The fall of lemuria and atlantis was a particularly traumatizing time for our souls. It created a great rift for many beings, shattering them and scattering them across the cosmos.

For a time, those controllers once used our unconscious collective pain around the fall of atlantis to torment us blindly. Since we couldn't remember our Atlantean and Lemurian and previous connections, we experienced feelings of disembodied trauma without knowing why consciously.

**What Happened? To Atlantis and Lemuria**

This is a view I will share that my soul wants to share. It has wanted to share this for a while to spread the truth.

There was a great betrayal. A betrayal of our very souls. The beings we trusted to be our brothers, our kindred spirits betrayed us for the equivalent of a few coins.

I, the author, specifically remember being betrayed, and as a result, something I created killed millions of people in an instant. It is a pain my soul wore for millennia, until I was able to come to a place of inner forgiveness. I share this with you now, a memory once hidden and used to torment me, I am now able to see.

Many of us carry similar seeds.

It tore us from our very fabric within, and sent us on a downward spiral into over 30 thousand years of torment and enslavement within our very beings.

Many of us feel the pain of this betrayal and separation very acutely.

You will notice, we don't have evidence of that technology. It was all destroyed, in conjunction with keeping us in the dark, literally and figuratively.

**The Healing of Atlantis and Lemuria timelines**

The story is not all dark. Here and now, a beautiful rainbow has arose from all that has happened and all that is.

We are that rainbow, a variety of frequencies, colors, textures, and resonances, that came forth from across time and space to rejoin here and now. We knew this moment would come, and so right now, at the time of writing this book and by the time you read it, we are integrating our old 'pains' from our Atlantis and Lemuria lifetimes.

In those lifetimes, we experienced catastrophe. For a time after that, we have been sitting somewhat 'unresolved' as though we were in a perpetual cliffhanger. That time of resolution is now. There is nothing you need to struggle for or figure out. Allow yourself to be reconnected to this time, to this energy. Be sovereign as you hold space for yourself.

If this resonates with you, I suggest taking some time to sit in nature, with yourself, and speak to your heart. Ask it to show you what wants to be loved. Observe without judgement, then love unconditionally whatever emerges.

### Are we going back to Atlantis? To Lemuria?

In the fullest scheme of things, we may have cycles that seem to mirror previous cycles, but we never really 'move back'

All experiences are a cumulation of all we have learned up until this point.

You might say "earth" was running several probabilities of the best case scenario, and now we've just about found it and are collapsing the timelines to line up to the present moment.

Where we are headed is something similar to Atlantis, Lemuria and other great civilizations - but it is also something completely unique and new.

It is like all the best and brightest minds in all of creation, in all of the universe are here on this Earth now.

It's as though we're taking all the best, from all the scenarios we have run, and we have placed them and are placing them into this moment.

# From the highest perspective,

**The controllers, the light and dark, are all aspects of ourselves:**

Here is a metaphor for the perspective of what happened from universal source:

You might say, we were a singularity, that became a 'group' and then that group decided to split up and each contribute to the story. "I will be the 'bad" guy" one said. "I will be the victim" another said. "I will be the hero" another said. We all thought this was a fascinating idea, and then said "Also, for the sake of keeping it interesting, let's switch up our roles now and then, and try all the experiences there are to try. Let's be the light sometimes and the dark sometimes. It will be fun"

We added the experience of 'death' so that roles could be ended when their experience was done, so we could really engage with the experience.

**Then, something unexpected happened: we got really good at the game. So good, that we tricked ourselves.**

We were determined to create an answer to the question - Can the all powerful divine create a situation where they forget their divinity - and then find their way back?

In order to find out that answer, we created a situation where we could pull ourselves to the limits - the 'battle of dark and light.'

When the limits were pressed far enough, we made a choice and engaged a sort of 'fail safe' by choosing to have a mass incarnation of high consciousness beings at this point in time, to facilitate a mass ascension process that would ensure the return to zero point balance.

**Is there a battle of light and dark? Do we need to fight for our freedom from the controllers?**

Earlier I mentioned a battle of light and dark. I talked about controllers, I talked about timelines and wars.

Well, I have some uplifted news. For one, there is no more battle to be fought. For all intents and purposes it is won - or rather, it no longer exists, beyond what individuals choose to focus on.

There are no more controllers who have power over you. The false grid has been dismantled. This is a moment of reclaiming, remembering, and recollection. You have the choice now to step forward from any self-imposed cages. No one can call you their master. You are now open to step forward and claim your rightful seat at the throne of your awareness.

The way we ALL win - the light AND the dark - It is to not fight it within ourselves. When we fight as the light or the dark, it is irrelevant which side we are on. The moment we take sides, we are split - polarized. And it doesn't matter if a side (temporarily) wins or not - what keeps darkness in power is the focus on separation. It is the energy of conflict itself that the darkness seeks. Because no matter how many battles are fought, as long as conflict and separation exists, it would be able to continue.

Therefore fighting darkness is at its core a lost cause.

So what is the true answer? Integration and unconditional love. Forgiveness. Understanding that the 'other', no matter how hateful they seem, is really just an aspect of you that is in temporary confusion.

Please note, this is not a suggestion to place yourself in a harmful position or engage with people who might attack you. Remember, they are deep in their story. The way you can help shift all of life, begins within. How you see them. Do you battle within yourself? Or do you find the place of peace and integration within?

Again, **There is no more war currently, other than our skirmishes within**

If you are reading this book, you are in a timeline where there has already been a critical mass tipping point towards ascension. That means, we are all on an ascension path. It is not a 'light or dark' winning path - it is an ALL UNIFYING path.

Those who were the controllers are not to be condemned or hated - for in reality, they are our brothers and sisters in disguise. They willingly chose to embody this path at higher dimensional levels, just as we did, knowing what that meant for them. The way we free them, as well as ourselves, is will unconditional love, and focusing on how they can be integrated back into the whole.

So, don't be fooled by displays of darkness, nor by calls to 'fight for the light.' The darkness is not gone, it is being called to be integrated in all that is. That is how the shift has happened, and how it continues to happen.

As we embrace the darkness AND light within us all, without judgement, there is no more battle. Only complete acceptance. And that is how ALL of us truly win.

# Paving the Way for Living Your Utopia Here On Earth:

## And living what you were meant to live through forgiveness and unity

That explanation of our current ascension timeline is one perspective.

But what would be the full perspective of why we chose to live this life? Just moments ago, I mentioned that we are not meant to condemn those who did harm.

Why is that? Because, in our highest, fullest perspectives, it was and is all a unified choice.

We chose to live life for the experience of it. All of it - the perceived good and bad. The up the down, the light the dark.

Now, I'm going to speak in terms of 'before and after'. Understand that these concepts don't fully translated in this way, but it will do for now.

Before we had creation, there was only oneness. This is sometimes hard for us to imagine, because the mind lives in duality. There can be no ultimately oneness from the perspective of the mind. Your heart, however, can understand this concept.

You can understand the concept of oneness when you are in states of supreme love, supreme joy. When you're so connected to the present moment, to the person or people you are with, to nature, whatever it is. When you're in deep meditation. It feels like time stands still, and every cell in your body feels alive and electrified.

You feel a greater connection to all that is. This is what so many of us spend all our lives searching for. We keep looking externally to ourselves, because we mistake the symptoms of happiness and wealth (external experience) for TRUE happiness and wealth (inner wholeness).

There's no judgement in this statement, nor is it necessary to judge ourselves for chasing things externally. We chose to come forth, and experience this magnificent creation for ourself.

You see, at our highest levels, we are source. Universe, divinity, god, whatever you want to call it. Our true nature is that.

So why do we seem separate? It's the delusion of illusion. In order to create a simulation of separation, we did a sort of 'vibratory illusion.'

From source, a 'point outside' was created. Remember, this was all perspective, for there could be nothing outside of totality. But totality 'pretended' that there was. This outside point was the spark of creation.

This spark 'went out' from the center, pulling away from the source.

This pull away from source that is contrasted by source attempting to pull it back creates the vibration that is the building blocks for all of creation.

This vibration is known as the OM or AUM sound.

From this place, there became 2 points. With 2 points, you were suddenly able to create measurements between the two points. This created 'space and time' - the distance and how long it took to travel between the distances.

As more points were added, different vibrations were created, relative to the perspective it was observed from. With all this variation, we had the different 'materials' - the atoms that were the vibrating building blocks of life.

**Creation - which we will call Source - wanted to experience itself**

And so, life was created. Specks of dust swirled and became stars, solar systems, universes. Microcosms formed within macrocosms, creating life on all levels of existence.

And in every single particle of existence, is the awareness of source.

Again, all of life is being experienced by source through every particle, every animal, every human alive.

The idea of separation is a distortion, created by having duality. Because we have good and bad and light and dark, we have contrast. And because we have contrast we can have Unified and Separated.

All of life therefore, is a paradox, in that it is both in a state of existence and non existance, it happens in time, it has already happened, and it is all happening right now. It is light and it is dark- and it is ultimately everything and nothing.

This delicate balance is perfectly held in place by universal wisdom. The yin yang of energy always compliments each other. Even in chaos there is order, and even in order there is chaos.

For a while, creation was focused on the highest good. Ideas like destiny existed. Experiences emerged forth that were guided by divine will. However, after a few millenia of this, source wanted to experience everything there was to experience.

So source would 'split' itself. It would multiply these opposing forces and give them free will.

A way you might picture this, is if you wrote a computer program to have a certain algorithm that would cause it to learn and adjust as it went. Then once you hit 'start' you would no longer control it until it returned back to you on its own free will. This is one way to explain the concept behind free will.

**Earth - the planet designed with Free Will**

One of the things that made and makes earth fascinating, is that it was designed and intended to be a place of free will.

We are considered a significant planet to the ascension process, as we're 'leading the way.' Many other planets are waiting for us to complete our process to follow suit.

Earth herself is a sentient being who chose to support life on her for this drama experiment, experience. She is a higher dimensional being at her core herself.

She is such a being of unconditional love, that she has chosen to be gentle in her ascension process, to give everyone the chance to make their free-willed choices, whether they choose to stay an ascend, or leave the body to go elsewhere.

When I say leave the body, I am talking about death. And there are some choosing to die at this time of ascension. Understand, death from the fullest dimensional awareness is not a punishment nor something we would mourn. From a multidimensional level, it's like how we view changing clothes here.

**Noting the Paradox between real and not real in this conflict:**

In the fullest perspective, from source perspective, all of life and all of creation was and is source playing a large scale game of life and death with ourselves.

Please note, this is not meant to wave the hand or diminish the incredible saga that unfolded from the experience.

It can be easy and lofty to say "Pain isn't real" and "All of creation is an illusion" which is true from one perspective - however when we speak from that perspective, we're talking from an 11th-12th+ dimensional perspective.

We are currently experiencing reality in 3d-5d+. It serves no one to gloss over the experiences that all of us in unity created, experienced, and are experiencing. In fact, ignoring our feelings is one of the things that gets us 'caught up' in the drama time to time.

The truth is, even if it is not real, we are and have been experiencing it as real for the duration of our existence here on creation, with brief glimpses of the freedom and wholeness we are.

Our experience of it being real makes it real for us. When this happens, it is important to honor the experience, and the perspective of the experiencer, while drawing the focus towards what wants to be created. (Honor it, without getting enmeshed in the story) It's certainly a fine line we walk. (We'll have more materials that cover how you can approach this near the end of the book)

# Awakening From Slumber:

**The Cycle of Ages, Where we are now, and where we are headed**

You may have noticed things have gotten shaken up recently, especially around 2012. Not just externally, but much of your internal self has shifted as well.

In order to explain this phenomenon, and to chart out where we came from and where we are headed, we're going to use the Hindu explanation of the "Yugas'

(Author's note: As a child growing up, I studied Sri Yukteswar's Yuga explanation in "The Holy Science." For the purpose of this discussion, we will use his explanation here. I would note that all things are subjective, especially when discussing time, so rather than getting too focused on specific dates and numbers, to use these time markers as general points for building your understanding, not as unbendable facts)

A Yuga is a measurement of time that spans 24,000 years. [Sri Yukteswar's] theory is based on the idea that the sun "takes some star for its dual and revolves round it in about 24,000 years of our earth – a celestial phenomenon which causes the backward movement of the equinoctial points around the zodiac."

In other words, the explanation is that as the Earth and the sun move through the different celestial bodies over the course of thousands of years, each of these celestial bodies creates an influence on the experience of life here on earth.

You can see here a depiction of the yugas. The artist included astrological symbols in the inner circle as well. (Copyright free share use via Wikipedia)

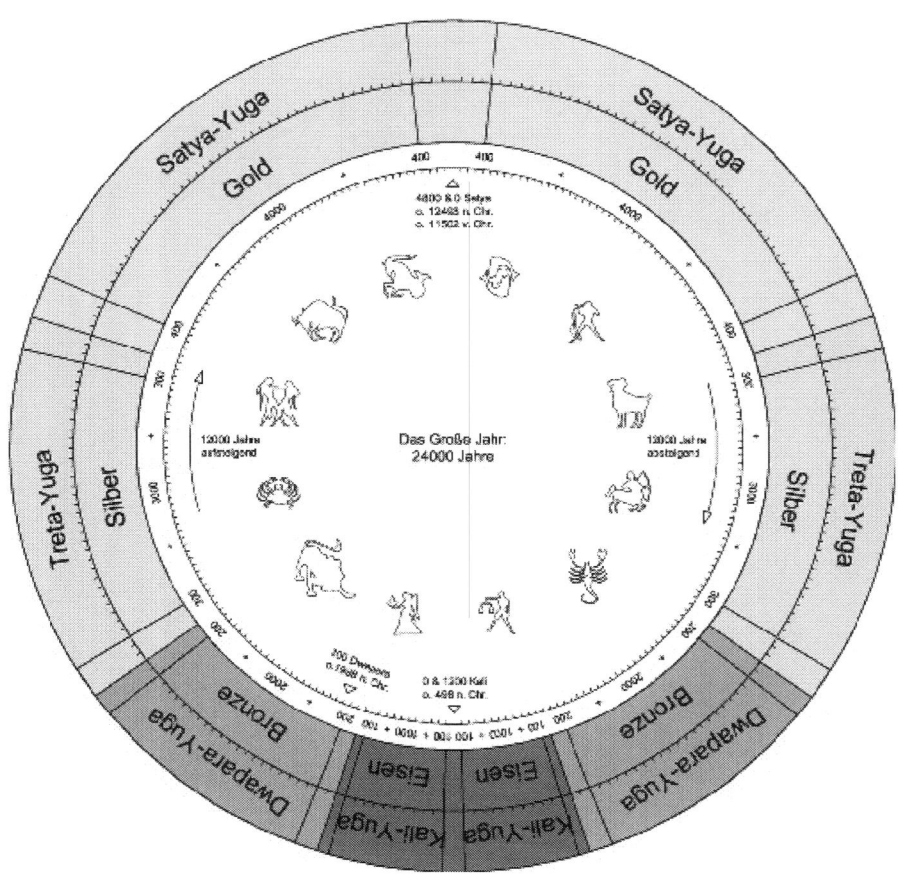

# What are the different ages?

If we follow the yuga chart, we can see there are golden ages, silver ages, bronze ages, and iron ages.

- The golden ages are said to be when consciousness is its most aware.

- The silver ages are ages of advancement

- The bronze ages are ages of industry

- The iron age is the darkest age with the least awareness.

We are currently said to be right around the end of the bronze age, heading into the silver, in an ascending (rising) direction.

This means we are rising in consciousness.

Here is a more detailed description pulled from the wikipedia page on the yugas:

## Characteristics of each Yuga

- Satya Yuga (also known as Krita Yuga "Golden Age"): The first and best Yuga. It was the age of truth and perfection. The Krita Yuga was so named because there was but one religion, and all men were saintly: therefore they were not required to perform religious ceremonies. Humans were gigantic, powerfully built, honest, youthful, vigorous, erudite and virtuous. The Vedas were one. All mankind could attain to supreme blessedness. There was no agriculture or mining as the earth yielded those riches on its own. Weather was pleasant and everyone was happy. There were no religious sects. There was no disease, decrepitude or fear of anything. Human lifespan was 100,000 years and humans tended to have hundreds or thousands of sons or daughters. People had to perform penances for thousands of years to acquire Samadhi and die.

- Treta Yuga: (Silver) Is considered to be the second Yuga in order, however Treta means the "Third". In this age, virtue diminishes slightly. At the beginning of the age, many emperors rise to dominance and conquer the world. Wars become frequent and weather begins to change to extremities. Oceans and deserts are formed. People become slightly diminished compared to their predecessors. Agriculture, labour and mining become existent. Average lifespan of humans is around 1000-10,000 years.

- Dvapara Yuga: (Bronze) Is considered to be the third Yuga in order. Dvapara means "two pair" or "after two". In this age, people become tainted with Tamasic qualities and aren't as strong as their ancestors. Diseases became rampant. Humans are discontent and fight each other. Vedas are divided into four parts. People still possess characteristics of youth in old age. Average lifespan of humans is around a few centuries.

- Kali Yuga: (Iron) The final age. It is the age of darkness and ignorance. People become sinners and lack virtue. They become slaves to their passions and are barely as powerful as their earliest ancestors in the Satya Yuga. Society falls into disuse and people become liars and hypocrites. Knowledge is lost and scriptures are diminished. Humans eat forbidden and dirty food. The environment is polluted, water and food become scarce. Wealth is heavily diminished. Families become non-existent. Average lifespan of people is barely 100 years, though, by the end of the Yuga, it will be as low as 20 years

# The 2012 Awakening Catalyst

Right now, we are at the brink of transition from the bronze age to the silver age.

Starting since around 2012, we begin the transition or ascension process. You might have noticed many "Mayan calendar prophecies' around this point.

You were also likely aware in your own life that around this time, that things started to radically shift for you. That is because you were activated, and your very vibration begun to shift. All the things that were not in alignment with your ascension path begun to fade away.

You began to draw things into your life that would begin to remind you of who you truly were.

If you stop and consider this for a moment, you might notice that around 2012, life changed radically for you in one or more ways.

What about the 'doomsday' predictions?

There was a sort of 'end of days' event that has happened and that is happening right now. It is the end of the days of the 3D control cycle.

It's not an armageddon prophecy, or an expectation of fire to rain from the skies.

In this case, we're experiencing the inner deaths of the stories of who we were, while we embrace the embodiment of who we truly are.

**Other timelines had World destruction - But we chose not to go that path**

There are other timelines that had existed that resulted in many loss of human lives, the end of the world as we know it, and even world destruction. I mention this, because sometimes people talk of doom and gloom, and wonder if that is where we are headed.

From this perspective, that is not the current timeline we are focused on.

How do I know this? Because you and I are talking here in this way right now.

Where we focus is what we choose. And we are choosing to focus on the creation of this new and exciting unified creation.

It is more than focus and choice, the collective has spoken through vibration. We are anchored deeply on our ascending trajectory here and now.

The more you focus on unity, within yourself, and within all of this creation you experience around you, the more connected you are to the outcome that sees everyone experiencing their fullest joy.

This is why it is of the utmost importance to nurture your focus and where you place your attention. What you resist will persist. What you embrace becomes merged into the full power of all you are.

There is nothing to fear in these words, and even if you do find yourself resisting, it's all well. You are connected and indeed a part of the well being of the whole universe. The more you let go of judgements and stories, the more you observe from a place of neutrality, the easier you will find your next aligned step from wherever you are now.

In other words, you're right where you need to be - so chill out and don't take this too seriously. You came for the ride of it all. Relax into the moment, and feel your wisdom emerge. It is here and now.

**This cycle is completely New - even for ancient souls**

As you're here reading this, I invite you to feel the truth of this statement:

We've been around this wheel more than once, but this time is something deliciously new. There is nothing 'mundane or normal' about this transition or transcendence.

Your connections to Ancient Civilizations. How you feel 'alien' sometimes or like you want to go back home.

You came here at this time, an advanced consciousness being, to help ground earth, all her children and all those living on her, and help during this tremendous shift.

When I say advanced here, it's not something to get 'ego excited' over. It simply means you have a different set of vibrations that helps during times of shift.

We are not above or below anyone else. We are each playing our role so the shift is easeful for all involved.

However, you ARE an incredible and valuable being. Each of us is. Each of us is needed in this time. That need to feel special and important is really our hearts and souls trying to wake us into remembering the truth of what we are.

We sometimes try to find that in external places and external sources, but it really is a homing signal trying to guide us within.

As you continue to read this book, you will find more tools and resources to help you understand and awaken to these signals in a way that is loving and helpful to you.

Know that you have come here by choice, and that you are an integral part of this whole. You are needed, and whether or not you understand 'what you are doing' - you are necessary for this shift, and you are indeed doing your part.

Consider reading this line a form of confirmation. If you were not, you would not have found this book, and you would not have read this passage.

**How to Ride the Crest of This Transition:**

The most powerful way we can ride the crest of this transition is with complete and unconditional love, beginning within with ourselves and radiating outwards to encompass all.

We've been told before that we need to push away parts of ourself, or only focus on positivity.

While well-meaning, this information ultimately leads to self confusion and self separation.

The kindest and most empowering choice you can make is to love yourself unconditionally and embrace all feelings and experiences that come up, as they come up.

# The steps for Emotional Integration are as follows:

1.  Willingness-Choice to feel and see the emotion

2.  Awareness and identification of the emotion without judgement

3.  Appreciation gratitude for the emotion

4.  Listening/analysis/receiving of the emotion without 'trying to make it change'

5.  Allowing/integration 'sitting' with the feeling and letting it be as it is

1) Be willing to take these steps. Make a choice that you're going to consciously engage in this process the best you know how.

2) Be aware of the feeling. Sometimes it helps to give it a name. "I feel anger. I feel confused." And so forth. There is no need to judge. You are simply labeling the feeling so you can clearly identify it.

3) Appreciate the feeling and thank it for showing up. This is challenging for some at first, but consider this: The feeling is a signal. Very much like a nerve on your body telling your brain that 'something is up.' Thank this feeling, thank this signal for working properly so that you can explore what it is signaling to you.

4) Sit with the feeling and listen to its message. You can use meditation, writing, sitting, whatever helps you clear your mind and focus on the feeling and receiving the message. Remember, you're not trying to change the feeling. You're allowing it to be as it is.

5) Allow the feeling to be as it is, until it shifts naturally. Remember, you're not trying to change the feeling. All that is necessary is to allow the feeling to be as it is without judgement

from a place of observation. In doing this, the feeling will naturally communicate and transmute, without you forcing it to change. Because you do not resist how you feel, you remain grounded, even if you experience great pain.

The feeling will either shift immediately, or you will feel a sense of allowing things to be as they are.

The key here, is you are no longer trying to 'bypass' the feeling. Instead, you are seeing your feelings as forms of communication that are a part of the whole of you. In embracing the feeling as it is, your relationship with the feeling and with your whole life changes from one of resistance to one of wholeness.

This is integration.

You will find your feeling around feelings shifts as you incorporate this process in your life, and it will become first nature for you.

Additionally, the more you forgive yourself and all of the world for the experience, the more you come to a place of inner peace and allowing. In this space, you will remember ultimately we are all love. The only time we act outside of that love is when we're temporarily confused. Forgiving ourselves and others acts as a catalyst to transmute pain into awareness, and then helps us remember there was nothing to be upset about all along, as we were all in this play of life together.

# Closing thoughts on moving forward

All of this is meant to be a perspective for you on what has come to pass and what has brought us here.

I feel inspired to create this book one midsummer's day (well, closer to mid august)

I knew one day, it would help us with the disclosure we're currently experiencing.

When this book is first released, it wouldn't surprise me if for a while it goes relatively unnoticed.

I know, in its time, it will help those who find it make sense of their newly awakened view on reality, and begin to piece together what is true for them.

Ultimately, this book isn't written to create sides, to condemn one group or build up another.

I wrote it so that we could ultimately remember, we came here to this world TOGETHER, UNITED, to have an experience.

All of us here are alive during the most exciting time of our life. It is a GIFT to be here, even when we're going through some of the most challenging changes in our life.

That's because what we're now about to create is unlike anything else this world or even this universe has ever seen.

I always say to people, if you could be at the beginning, to throw your two cents into the primordial pool, wouldn't you want to?

And really, that is what we're all doing here, by living our lives in whatever way they're unfolding.

We ARE the soup of this fantastic new creation, and each of us is adding something completely fantastic, something completely unique.

We couldn't be this world in this way if we didn't all join in it together.

The key to remember, is there is no more war to fight.

There may be some chaos still. There may even seem like there's 'bursts of turmoil' here and there.

But if we've learned anything from the last several hundred thousand years of our evolution, it is that fighting and resistance only creates more of that which we are fighting and resisting.

The new way is alchemy - that is to say, the embracing and integration of all that is in the present moment, while we direct our focus on what we want to create.

By fully and unconditionally loving what is, all the situations, people, events, and so forth, we shift power from being projected outside of us, to remembering our power within.

The world we all want to see, that beautiful vision of joy and wonder that we KNOW exists, is being born in each moment.

When you love all people without exception, when you show tolerance and forgiveness, when you are compassionate in the face of hatred and fear, you are shifting this world.

All forms of seeming evil and darkness are part of this creation. We do not get anywhere by fighting it. We get somewhere when we stop resisting it, when we are compassionate with it, and when we shift our focus to what we DO want to create.

As you step forward into your life, ask yourself the question:

What do I want to focus on? What vision of life do I want to see?

And more importantly... how does it FEEL to live that life right now?

And when you ask yourself, feel how it feels. Embody it within and you will experience it without.

Thank you.

# About Danielle Lynn and Further Reading and Resources

Danielle Lynn is a teacher of self-awakening, emotional mastery, inner voice awareness and soul alchemy: transformation and transmutation at the soul level that transforms base energy into gold through the very core of your being.

She focuses on transformation with unconditional self love, as we are internal to external creators and all change is an internal to external flow that begins with you. She currently is writing several books to assist with the ascension process and shares regular inspirational messages and videos on her website.

If you feel a call to work with Danielle, or learn from her work, we invite you to visit and explore the following links and offerings below. Love you now and always.

To connect with Danielle, send a message, set up an interview, or book her to speak at your workshop or event, inquire at love@daniellelynn.com or at http://daniellelynn.com/contact

Read more articles at the blog http://daniellelynn.com/blog/

Visit our shop for courses, tools and other offerings http://daniellelynn.com/love-shop/

Add Danielle on facebook https://www.facebook.com/DanielleLynnCreate

Add Danielle on instagram https://www.instagram.com/dragonatplay/

To tune in to her videos visit here: https://www.youtube.com/channel/UC2x4T0BsrEIF-CPLUKNwdzw

***Additional Resources by other Authors:***

Extra reading by other authors on topics covered in this book can be found here if you feel inspired to delve deeper into the topic (note, Danielle does not endorse all the articles on these sites, it is a 'wild west' source, please use your discernment and choose what inspires your heart)

History of Earth: https://www.bibliotecapleyades.net/esp_historia_humanidad.htm

DNA Exploration: http://www.crystalinks.com/anunnakidna.html

Made in the USA
Middletown, DE
05 September 2018